Calman Revisited

MEL CALMAN

Calman
Revisited

METHUEN

This collection first published in 1983 by
Methuen London Ltd
11 New Fetter Lane, London EC4P 4EE

Bed-sit first published in book form by Jonathan Cape Ltd 1963
'Troubles with my Aunt' first appeared in the
Daily Telegraph Magazine 1974
Calman & Women first published by Jonathan Cape Ltd 1967
'The Resident' first published in *The Penguin Mel Calman* 1968
Couples first published in book form by The Workshop 1972
The new Penguin Calman containing the above first published by
Penguin Books Ltd 1977
Dr Calman's Dictionary of Psychoanalysis first published by W. H. Allen
Ltd 1979

The layout for the first part of this book was
designed by Philip Thompson

ISBN 0 413 52720 4

Printed in Great Britain by
Fletcher & Son Ltd, Norwich

*To my brother with love
and to Professor Kreplach with ambivalence*

Introduction

This collection is a mixture of various books I have produced over the last twenty years. They range from simple single cartoons (*Bed-sit*) to more complex attempts at deciphering male/female relationships (*Couples*). During these years I have slowly learned how to cope with the angst of having cartoon books published. I even published one book myself. This was *Couples*, which my gallery 'The Workshop' published when no proper publisher seemed very keen to do so. How they could overlook its evident merits is quite beyond me.

I learned a great deal from the experience, mainly about the enormous reluctance of some booksellers to part with money. I had the pleasure of seeing the book weighed in the palm of one of Britain's biggest wholesalers who said, 'Yes, it's good value for 50p – I'll take a thousand copies.' He did not look inside at the contents, which was my good luck, or he might not have liked it so much.

I will not bore the reader with long accounts of the genesis of each book. I think that the great S. J. Perelman once said that writing consisted of tearing up pieces of paper, and the same applies to cartooning.

I would like to say a few words, however, about *Bed-sit* because it marks the beginning of my relationship with the little man I draw. He turned up one day when he heard that the *Sunday Telegraph* had a single column box to let. I had, of course, seen glimpses of him before, but his real personality had been hidden from me. However, as soon as he found this room to live in, he seemed to make himself at home in my own life.

I realised that his views and opinions coincided in many ways with mine – but he had a neater way of expressing them. When I wanted to be angry, he preferred to shrug his shoulders and mutter some wry aphorism. Over the years since we first met in 1962, he has changed. He always looked middle-aged but now he really is middle-aged. His profile is more relaxed, less tense, and his clothes have become loose lines that could be half garment, half body.

When he gave up his box at the *Sunday Telegraph*, he tried living at *The Observer*. Unfortunately the editor, David Astor, expressed some bafflement at my man's so-called humour. He then visited *The Sunday Times* and found the atmosphere congenial: he even learned to be interested in politics and world affairs. He still doesn't understand them, but he hopes no-one apart from me notices that fact.

He now spends his weekdays at *The Times* and his Sundays at *The Sunday Times*. He even wanders abroad from time to time. I simply don't know how he manages to think of things to say. . . . I can only listen carefully and gratefully record them.

I don't know what I would do without him and I imagine he feels the same way about me.

Mel Calman
London, December 1982

Bed-sit

'Bed-sit' first appeared in the Sunday Telegraph *in 1962*

It may be small but the proportions are pleasing . .

Which is it to be today?
Toast and music,
toast and light,
music and toast in
darkness,
toast in silence?

*Have you
ever tried
to barbecue a
lamb chop
on a
gas ring?*

*The annoying thing about these rooms is that you
can almost overhear*

Some of my best friends are acquaintances

There comes a time in every bachelor's life
when he must say:
no more beans on toast –
and mean it

My position is roughly
left of coward . . .

They call me
the
St Francis
of
Earls Court . . .

Ah! La dolce vita . . .

The landlady doesn't like the word 'restrictions'. She calls them 'aids to communal living'

*I usually go
to the
launderette
in Kensington –
you meet a
better class
of dirty
washing there*

*That's funny – I didn't
know they
even knew each other*

*I could be
very
dominating –
if only
someone
would
volunteer to
be submissive . . .*

*I think I'll
ring
the office
and say
I'm dead . . .*

*I like to give the suit
an airing
from time to time*

*The girl next door
never seems to run out
of anything*

*I think I'll
do
a little
light
worrying . . .*

*These classical writers
really understood the
human predicament . . .*

*But I
asked
them to mine*

The score is
highly gratifying:
Christmas cards sent: 30
Christmas cards received: 32

Paper hat, yes.
Balloon, yes.
Bottle, yes.
Now let revelry commence . . .

Gentleman with artistic tastes
and cold feet
wishes to meet lady with
property in Bermuda . . .

*We depressives
are entitled
to a little bit
of manic
now and then . . .*

Troubles with my Aunt

1. *Paper Bags*

My aged Aunt saves paper bags. I don't mean that she puts one or two away in a drawer for a rainy day. We all do that. I mean she keeps every single paper bag that comes into the house. She unwraps the bread and carefully puts the bag in a drawer. She places the bags from the groceries in the same drawer. She has a system: the brown bags in one drawer and the white bags in another drawer.

She usually puts the small bags inside the largest bags, to save space. Bags lie on top of bags. Bags nestle inside bags. Bags beget bags. Whole communes of bags live inside those kitchen drawers.

I ask my Aunt, when I feel slightly frayed by all this bag cupidity, why she keeps all these bags. 'I need them,' she says, and the subject is closed. To be fair to her, she does use some of the bags. Let me explain.

Every night my Aunt prepares her bedtime tray. This tray is a ritual, an appeasement to the gods of sleep. The pink tray is placed beside the kitchen sink. My Aunt carefully takes three cups and half-fills them with cold water. Always three cups, always the same three cups. And always half-full. Never three-quarters or five-eighths. Exactly half. They are half-full because my Aunt has worked out over the years that a half-cup is exactly the right amount she needs to ease her heartburn. She gets attacks of heartburn in the middle of the night and she drinks fruit salts for this. A full cup of fruit salts is too much of a good thing. And she needs this cure three times a night. Hence, the three cups.

Ah, you may ask, why not a jug and three empty cups? Or even, a jug and one cup, which then gets half-filled three times? Because, as my Aunt patiently explained to me once, this method is foolproof and ready for use. It's an instant heartburn kit. No messing about in the half-light, trying to half-fill cups.

I once bought a jug and tried to persuade her to change her system, and she gave me a long, level stare that said: Never meddle with the laws of nature . . .

What about the paper bags, you cry. How do the paper bags cure the heartburn? Has the man lost all sense of narrative shape and decency? No. The paper bags are carefully torn open, flattened and used to cover the cups (or half-cups) of water. Each half-cup has its own little nightcap of paper, held down by a rubber band. And of course, they are needed to keep the dust out. My Aunt doesn't want dust getting into her water. Who would?

The problem is that even with using three bags a night, my Aunt is stockpiling bags rather rapidly. The drawers are full. I'm thinking of buying her a suitcase to keep the rest of her collection. But my Aunt doesn't approve of suitcases. Dust gets into them, she says. She admits that dust even gets into drawers. Which is why she gets the bags out every other day and dusts them. Gives them a careful dust, and then returns them to their correct drawer.

I believe my Aunt keeps these bags the way other old people have pets. Something to care for and look after. Not much company, perhaps. But at least house-trained. And, thankfully, very quiet.

2. Depressions

My Aunt and I suffered a great deal from depression, mostly hers. When she felt depressed she would come into my room – where I was usually looking at a blank sheet of paper, hoping a joke would appear on it – and sigh.

'What's the matter, Auntie?'

'I feel terrible.'

'Take a tranquillizer.'

'Do you think I should? Who knows what's in them?'

'Neither of us knows. Just take one and you'll feel better.'

'It may make me feel worse.'

'You always take them, and you always feel better.'

'I don't think they're the same ones as the last ones the doctor gave me.'

'Of course they are . . .'

'How do you know?'

'They look the same. Green and black. With your name on the bottle.'

'They don't taste the same. Perhaps the chemist has given me the wrong pills.'

'Take one, please . . .'

Sigh. 'You think I should?'

'Yes, I do.'

'Doctors. What do they know?'

As my Aunt got older she suffered more and more from hypochondria (which must be hereditary, because I get it too – especially in the middle of the night) and needed more and more to consult doctors, in spite of her basic lack of faith in them.

Days would start and end with my Aunt asking me to call a doctor because she felt 'terrible'. If the doctor came, she would repeat all her ailments and troubles. He would listen patiently, leave a prescription, and I would go to the chemist with it.

Whatever was prescribed, my Aunt would distrust it. Look at it, sniff it, and worry whether it would make her worse. She would snort. 'What do doctors know? My mother, bless her, knew more in her little finger than these young kids know in their whole heads . . .'

'Why get me to call the doctor then?'

'What do you want me to do? Suffer in silence?'

Whatever else my Aunt did, she certainly never suffered in silence. She suffered her anxieties and depressions out loud. She crossed each day gingerly, as if it were a tightrope which might snap under her at any moment, and plunge her to her death.

The mornings began with sighs and remarks about how badly she slept the night before.

'I went to bed late again last night,' she would say.

'Really, why?'

'I started thinking about your mother and how she never looked after herself properly. If she had listened to me, she would still be alive. Always rushing about, doing things, enjoying herself. She should have rested her heart more.'

'Well, she did live to be seventy-eight. That's not too bad.'

'She could have lived another twenty years, if she had listened to me.'

'Her doctor said . . .'

'What do doctors know? Nothing.'

Then came breakfast of cups of tea and cream crackers. (Always Jacobs'. I once tried to palm her off with another brand and she sulked all day.) Then more sighs and heartburn. Treatment for heartburn with fruit salts, and more cups of tea.

More heartburn would follow the cups of tea. More anxiety would follow the heartburn.

'Do you think I've got an ulcer?' she would ask me, clutching her stomach.

'Of course not. But I shouldn't drink so much tea. It can't be good for your stomach.'

'Perhaps I should see a Specialist?'

'What kind of Specialist?'

'Someone who specializes in everything.'

'Just take a tranquillizer.'

'Do you think I should?'

'Yes, for God's sake, yes.'

'It might make me feel worse . . .'

How I wished there was a pill she could have taken to make her calm enough to take her tranquillizers . . .

3. Baths

Once a week my Aunt would announce, 'I am going to have My Bath today.'

Now most people find it fairly simple to have a bath. You probably remember how it goes. You enter the bathroom, you put the plug in, turn on the hot water, get into the bath, wash, sing, get out, dry yourself and exit. My Aunt's approach was more Epic, like one of those long Eisenstein movies where people seem to be forever climbing up the same flight of stairs.

My Aunt would first slowly collect her clean linen, so as to have it all ready for changing into after Her Bath. This involved Sorting Out her linen, which took up most of the morning. Sometimes she would find an old letter buried amongst her linen, become interested in the memories it aroused and have to postpone The Bath until the next day. But if all went well, she would have a bite of lunch and start Phase Two around two o'clock.

Phase Two was Washing Out the Bath. She had a great fetish about cleanliness, which I imagine was sexual in origin, since she was a maiden Aunt. I am sure Freud would have enjoyed analysing her motives – all I know is that it was very heavy on the Vim. She would wash the bath very thoroughly, rinse it with running cold water, rewash it and then carefully feel the whole surface with her fingers. If there was the slightest blemish, she would clean the whole bath out again. This took about an hour. Then she would fill the bath.

By this time she was feeling a bit hungry and exhausted. So she would put on the kettle for a cup of tea. Several cups of tea and several cream crackers (her favourite food) later, she would go back to the bathroom. And find the water stone cold.

So she would have to empty the bath and re-fill it. While it was filling, she would go to collect her Clean Linen. She carried all her underclothes carefully wrapped up in an old piece of torn sheet, tied and sealed with several safety-pins. I don't know why they had to be wrapped up like this since the distance between her bedroom and the bathroom was all of five yards. I think it was in case dust (one of my Aunt's great enemies) got at the clean linen.

At last she was actually ready for Phase Three – the Bath itself. Before she entered the water, she would call out to me that she was going in (in case I had not noticed she was Having a Bath) and that she was leaving the door unlocked in case she felt faint and needed sudden rescuing from drowning.

I would then settle down to work, and she would call out again. 'Can you shut the window? I can't lift it and I can't have a draught blowing down on me in the bath.' She always liked the window open whilst running the bath, to allow the gas fumes from the Ascot to escape, and she would always then need the window shut before she could enjoy the bath.

About an hour later she would slowly emerge from the steamy bathroom, carefully swathed in clean underwear and towels. (For some other deep Freudian reason unknown to me, my Aunt never owned, and could never be persuaded to buy, any kind of dressing-gown. I think she thought they were only worn by Loose Women.)

'Be a good boy,' she would say, 'and make me a nice cup of tea. I feel faint. The bath was far too hot.' Or sometimes it was, 'I feel faint and cold. I think I caught a chill in there.'

I would make us a pot of tea and she would drink it greedily, and sigh, as if just rescued from a sinking ship. She looked rather like a survivor, all wrapped in towels and exuding dampness. 'Thank God that's done,' she said. 'It's a terrible business, having a bath.'

Calman and Women

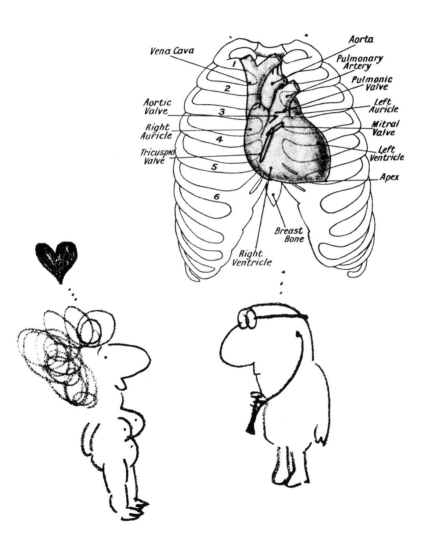

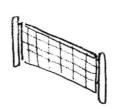

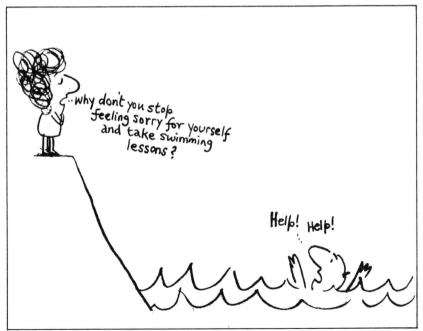

Don't bother
me now —
I've got a
lot on my
mind......

I think women need a sense
of purpose in life

..: Are you listening?

yes dear!

One man's meat
is another woman's
Sunday gone

But it's my turn
to leave you.

The last time
I went into one of
those it took me
five years to
get out...

well—

If I allow myself to love you
I will be vulnerable and you
might hurt me— anyway...
I can't relate to you whilst
I am dependent on you financially...
I need to be free and I need
to love myself before I can
love you... and my analyst says
that I am too anxious to love
anyone. I do love you, or rather,
I _want_ to love you but...
Perhaps I could go and live away
from you for awhile, then I might
be free to come closer to you,
if you see what I mean...
Oh dear! It's really not fair
of you to keep asking me
these difficult questions...

Do you love me?

The Resident

WELL—
I'm here...

I wonder what he wants
me to do...

no sign of any instructions..

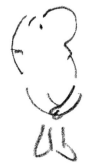

no message scrawled
in the dust..

It's really annoying —
I come here, I want to do
my best and
there's silence...

... Shall I dance?

Shall
I juggle?

or am I just going
to cope bravely
with life...

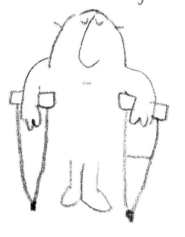

Condemned to my wheelchair...
resigned to my affliction..

Converting the
dross of pain
into the gold
of serenity...

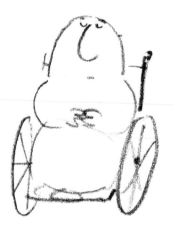

No thank you . . .

it's a good
part but I hate
long runs...

NOBODY KNOWS THE TROUBLE I'VE SEEN!
BUT - I'm soon going to remedy that...
FIRST!
I've got this backache which grips me suddenly as I walk along...
ACHE

THEN - I get these terrible
migraine headaches
once a month...

AND -
I don't sleep well -
if I get two or
three hours a
night I think
I'm lucky...

I just lie there worrying about the
money I owe and my
thinning hair...

AND THAT'S NOT ALL..

You see, basically I feel I'm not really enjoying life..

.. AND I worry about that.

The joke is-
I didn't ask to be
here.. I was
created..

And it's not
funny...

... HOW WOULD
YOU LIKE TO
BE THE FIGMENT
OF SOMEONE ELSE'S
IMAGINATION?

I just skipped a page and
he didn't notice!

.. AT LEAST –
I think he didn't notice...maybe
he intended me to skip a
page – part of some
terrible plot he's brewing...

You CANT
  trust anyone
these days!

Ever since writers gave up
happy endings I feel very
uneasy...

It's become fashionable to be
unhappy. I'm old-fashioned.
I say - and I mean it ...

BRING BACK THE HAPPY ENDINGS!

DOWN WITH DOSTOEVSKY!
LONG LIVE IVOR NOVELLO!

Let us remember—

BAD ART can be
GOOD FUN...

especially for us
poor souls who
have to sweat
it out..

day after day..

LIFT THAT ANGST!
TOTE THAT
PSYCHE!

Body & soul
racked with
pain...

SUDDENLY — I feel sad again..

I knew it was too good to last..

If he sees me enjoying myself he gets jealous...

WANTS ALL THE GLORY FOR HIMSELF...

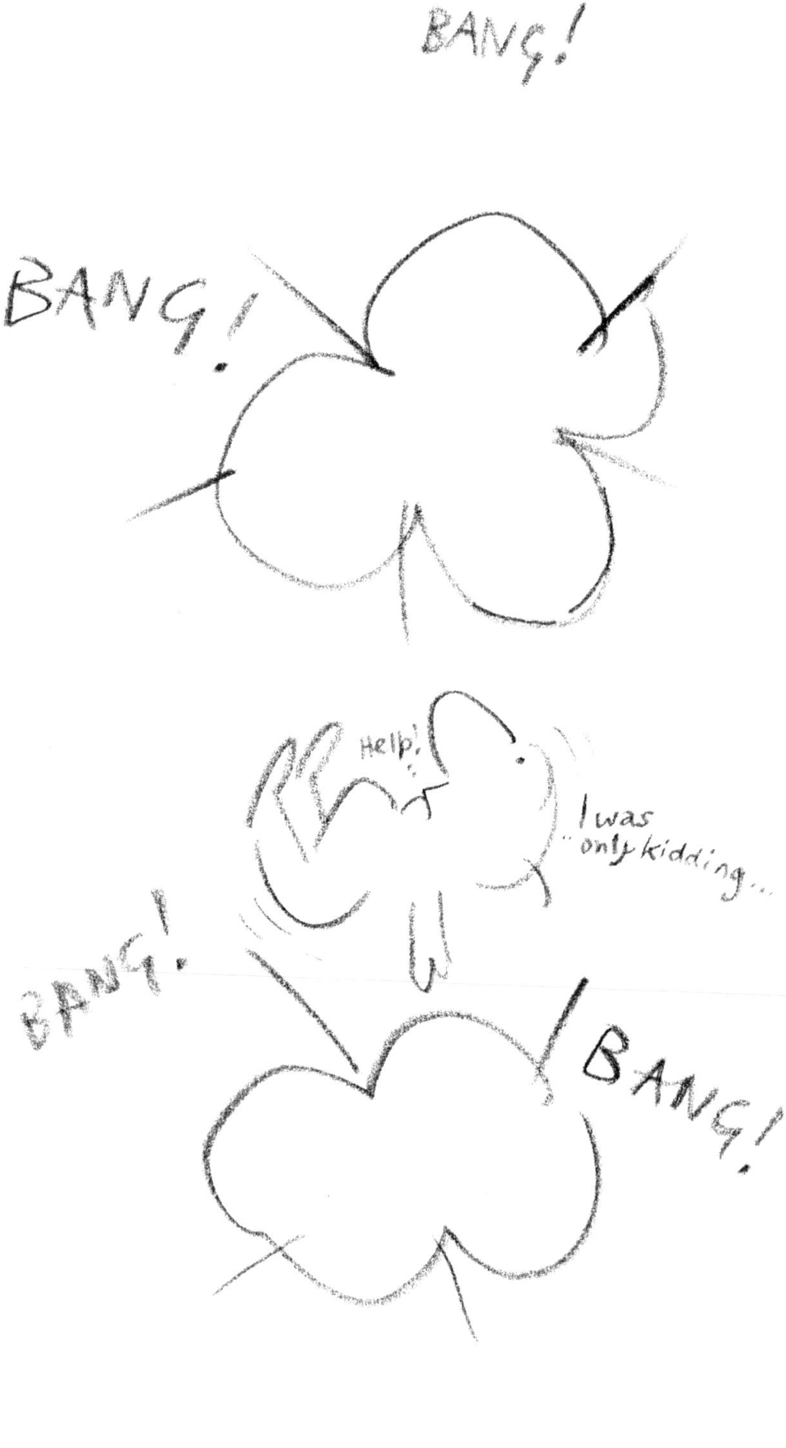
BANG!
BANG!
Help!
I was only kidding...
BANG!
BANG!

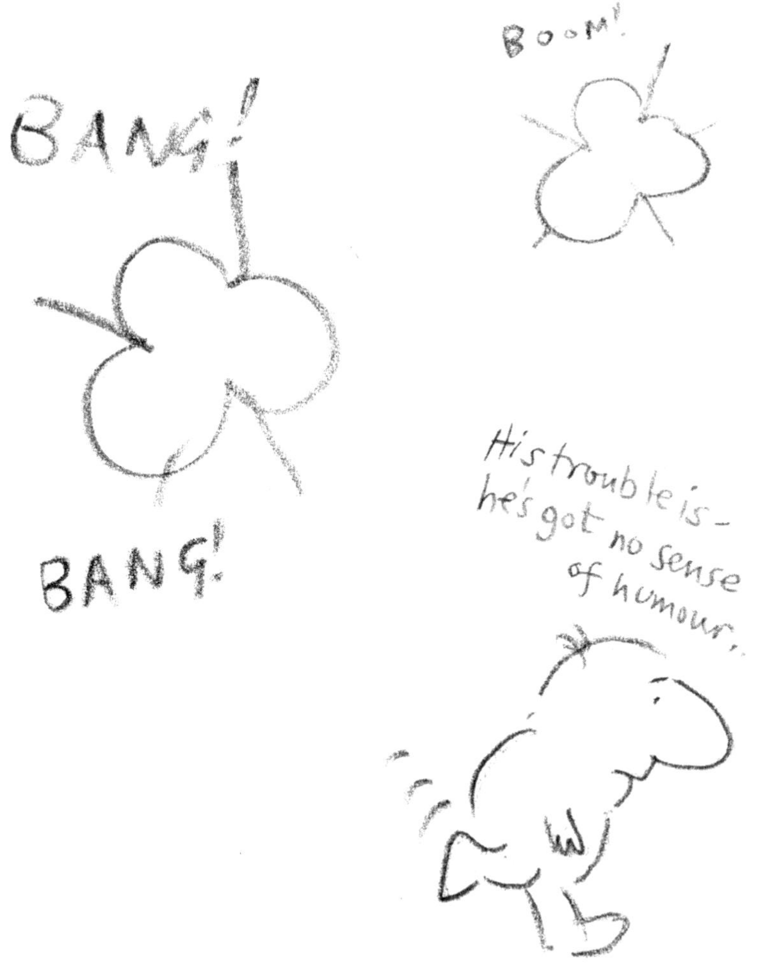

BANG!
BOOM!
BANG!
His trouble is - he's got no sense of humour.

I know what I'll do —

I'LL RESIGN !

That will teach
him to mess me
about ...

A dignified letter -

Dear Sir, I feel
the time has come for us
to part company. I have
long felt intense
dissatisfaction with
the living arrangements.
Either it's too cold or too hot. It
rains frequently. The food is
inadequate – the company
non-existent. The fantasies I have
are of poor quality. One is continually
promised improvements in all directions.
Change is always in the air but never
on the ground. Even the misery lacks
grandeur. There is a feeling of triviality
infusing all departments. Apathy
and ennui are my handmaidens. I
would have thought you would have
been ashamed of the poverty of the
inventions I inhabit. I feel ashamed

to be seen in them. Fortunately, few people see me in my reduced circumstances, for the general public has the good taste to avoid the ridiculous and the insignificant. I therefore wish to be excused further participation in this charade. Please consider me as no longer available. I resign. I quit. I won't move. I won't speak your words. I won't perform your actions. Thanking you for your interest, I remain,

Yours respectfully,

etc

etc

I think I just wrote myself out of a job..

- SILENCE -

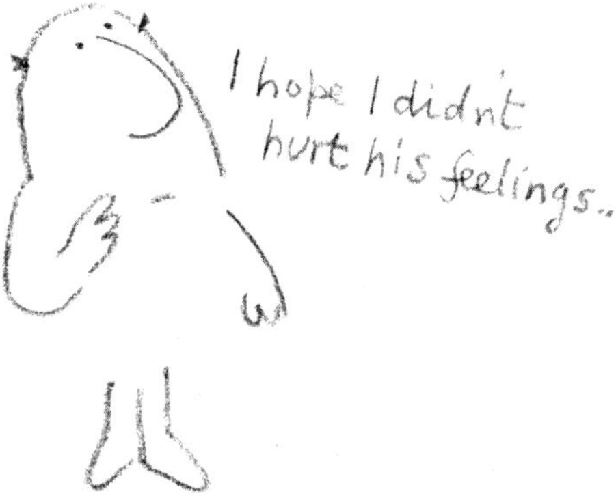

The great thing in this racket is to survive....

The next page may be better..

and if it isn't.. dont worry.. keep smiling.. count your blessings.. enjoy the little things.. if the text is lousy – admire the binding ...

As my mother used to say — if life hands you a lemon, make lemonade..

The trouble is —

lemonade gives me heartburn...

I see words ahead-
perhaps it's a message?
GOOD NEWS
AT LAST!
?
THE
END

?
The End? - is that a promise or a threat?
But I was just beginning to like it here...

THE
END

Couples

The idea of a double-decker strip cartoon is not entirely new: in the early 1900s George Herriman created a double strip about a cat and a mouse living underneath a family called 'The Dingbat Family'. Eventually the family were evicted and the strip became 'Krazy Kat'.

I've always been interested in the gap between what people say and what they think, and I felt that a two-level strip might be a good place to explore this gap. At first I put the thoughts above the characters (as in the usual think-bubble convention), but as I wanted people to read the thoughts after they'd read the spoken words, I finally placed the thoughts on the bottom layer. My thoughts always seem to me to be below my conscious mind.

Originally I wanted to draw the bottom level as a rather surreal landscape, which only connected with the top level at times, and at other times followed its own logic. But various readers' reactions (the strip ran for a year in the *Sunday Times*) made me realize this would be too complicated and confusing. So the strip settled into something more conventional than I had hoped for – governed by the tyranny of a punch line in the last frame. I suppose the ideal strip would run on without having to end in a gag – but that would be something else. I think it's called 'life'.

Do you think I'm manly?
MAN & THE COLOUR MAG
Yes, of course
SPORTS SECTION
What's your definition of 'manly'?
MAN &
SPORTS SECTION
8 for virility
9 for bossiness
8
9
it's any man who thinks I'm womanly
MAN &

Daydreaming again?
Fantasies are all very well, but I bet she can't cook as well as I can..
That's O.K. – you can do the catering...

What are you thinking?
Nothing..
If I catch you having sexual fantasies, I'll –
You'll what?
I'll join you...
?

That's it!
I'm going..
As soon as I start packing she'll ask me to stay..
Where's my blue shirt?
I don't know!
I'm packing! Say 'STAY'..
No!
I can't go without my blue shirt - so I'll have to stay
How to stay without losing face..'

Have you thought that marriage is just like tennis?
All that tension, drama, conflict of personalities, all that love going from side to side...
-Except that you always want to be the umpire as well...
Your fault!
She's right!
No-your fault!

Cooking! Cleaning! Why should women do it?
The natives are restless
WOMEN ARENT SLAVES
You're quite right
Peace!
WOMEN ARENT SLAVES
Let's get an au pair girl
Can I have one?
WOMEN ARENT SLAVES
FREE AU PAIRS NOW!

The butcher said I was beautiful today
SUNDAY TIMES
He says that to all his women customers
He also asked how my father was
Your father??
He meant you...

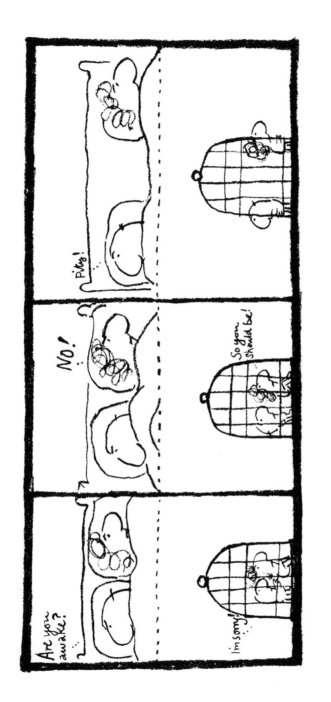

We can't afford it, and that's final!
Check! your move..
I'm going to bed –
If you're going to be like that – I'm not playing
– To SLEEP!
SLAM!
Stalemate!

Would you like to be buried with all your stuff - your Hi fi, your records...
TUTANKAN EXHIBITION
your back numbers of 'Playboy' - and me...
you?
UTAN
We could then spend eternity together...
Yes dear..
TUTANKAMEN EXHIBITION
Let me out! Now I know what the Pharoah's curse was...

How am I? I feel awful.. My back aches..
She's saying that to make me feel guilty for being away...
At least it can't be my fault because I'm not there..
How do you know it isn't aching because you're NOT here?
She should represent England at the Eurovision Last Word Contest...

Are you sleepy?
A bit
Shall we make love?
Maybe
I'm not sleepy!
What kind of answer is that?
It's a maybe I will or maybe I won't answer
I think I'll read for a while then
Come here or I'll rape you
Promises! Promises!

Dr Calman's
Dictionary of Psychoanalysis

Aggression

Ambivalence

Amnesia

Analyst

Anger

Animus & Anima

Anxiety

Which is it to be today?
Phobic, castration,
separation,
depressive,
paranoid anxiety
or plain
panic?

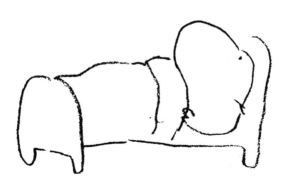

Bisexual

Breast

Castration Anxiety

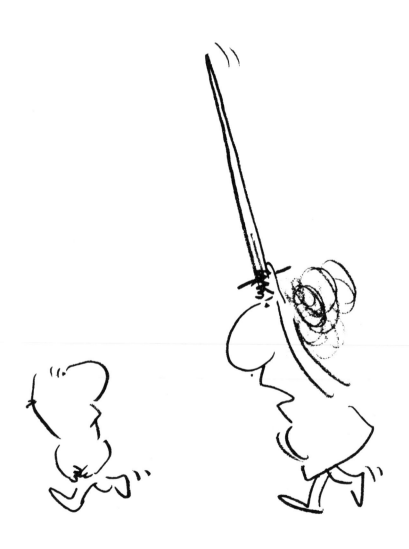

Claustrophobia

Coitus

Communication

One of my problems is that
I have trouble in communicating..
It seems I find myself using words
as a defence.. they are a shield
behind which I hide.. I don't believe
in the reality of feelings.. so I try
to verbalize my inner conflicts
and this results in a schizoid
dichotomy between my guts and
my head.. Do you follow me?
Do you find I cannot
communicate properly?
Well?

Compulsive

Conflict

This is either a bad case of conflict or a man with two wives: Editor.

Death Wish

Depression

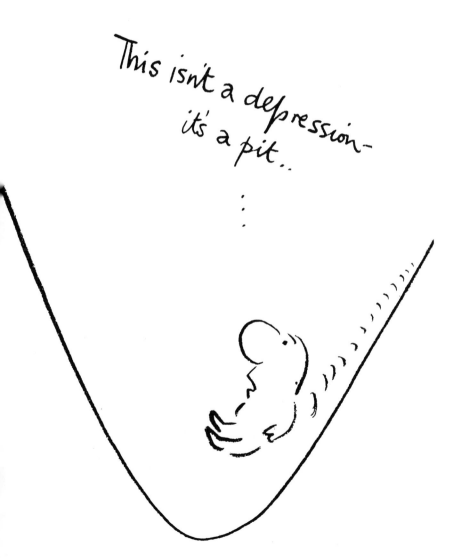

Dreams

Ego

Exhibitionism

Unfortunately, I'm only an ear, nose and throat chap — so I'll have to ask you to put your clothes on ...

Fantasy

Father

Fear

Fetish

For goodness sake - it has to be boots. Wellies won't do..

Fixation

my father...my father...

Forgetting

I don't care if it was unconscious - you shouldn't have forgotten my birthday..

Free Association

Freedom

Freudian Slip

Frigidity *(see Headaches)*

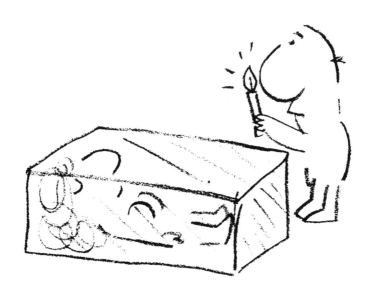

Gloom *(see Melancholia)*

Guilt

And now
I feel guilty
that I feel
so guilty
about everything

Happiness

What are the symptoms of happiness, Doctor?

Hate

Hostility

Hypochondria

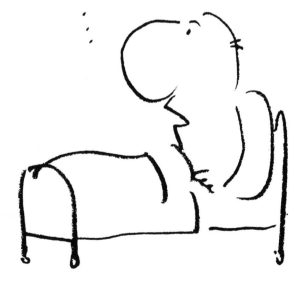

Even hypochondriacs get ill..

I

Id

Identity

Who am I?
I am ME. But is ME
really 'me' or just someone
who goes to an analyst
and has a wife and children
and his own overdraft?
And if I'm not me – who will
I be when I grow up... on the other
hand if I can keep away
from the cracks in the
pavements, I'll be
O.K... Please God.
If I believe in GOD...
whoever He is.. Oh god..
I'm late for my next
appointment..

Identity Crisis

Incest

She's not just old enough to be his mother - she is..

Infantile Regression

Insanity

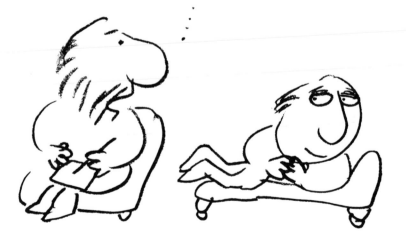

Jealousy

Libido

it's somewhere between your ID and your naughty bits ..

Love

When you say 'LOVE'
do you mean EROS or
a need for instinctual
satisfaction or object love
or oedipal love
or genital love
or simple old-fashioned
schmaltz?

Marriage *(see Help!)*

Doctor - I'm suffering from bouts of marriage..

Masochism

Masturbation

it's a bit boring
because I don't
fancy myself
all that much...

Mature

Melancholia *(see Depression)*

Mind

it's something
I'm always out of..

Mother *(see Oedipus Complex)*

Narcissism

Negative

Neurotic

Object

Obsession

The nature of obsession is very interesting. Obsessional thoughts express a need to control your impulses (see sex)... and I do wish you would wash your hands before you come next time as the germs tend to spread all over my couch and the next patient might contract your social diseases... now what was I saying?

Oedipus Complex *(see Mother)*

*If it wasn't for my mother -
I wouldn't be where
I am today ..*

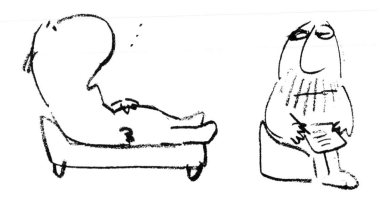

Orgasm

Paranoia

Patient

Penis Envy

Persona

Phallic Symbol

Phobia

Pleasure

Pleasure Principle

Projection

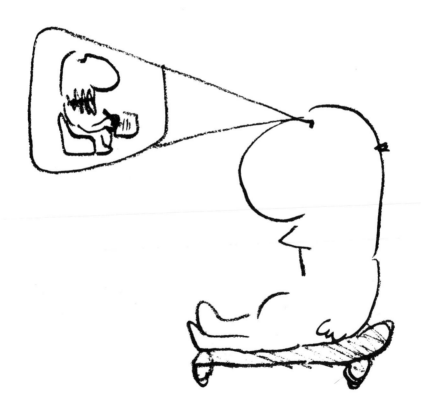

Psyche

Psychoanalysis

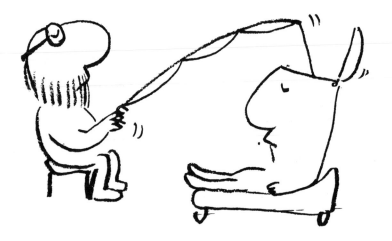

Psychosis

Psychosomatic

Rapport

Real

Reality

Religion

Repression

Sadness *(see Gloom, Depression)*

Separation Anxiety

No – I'm fine...
Just to say I'm at the airport...
I'm fine. Are you? Sure?
I know I just left but –
well.. I could cancel my trip
if you like.. I didn't want
to go.. but you said I should..
Anyway.. so long as you're
O.K.. I'll be back
tomorrow.. or maybe
before then...
Look – why don't you
come with me?
:..

Sex

Sexual Perversion

I dont mind dressing up as a chicken— but I'm damned if I'm going to lay eggs for her

Superego

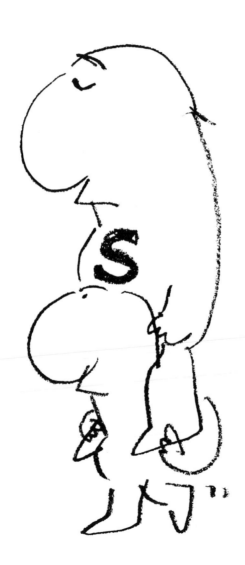

Time

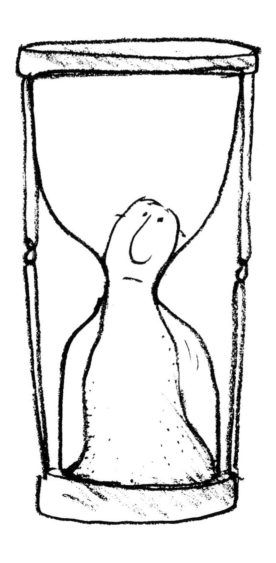

Transference

Transvestite

Trauma

I come from
a long line of

traumas..

Truth

Unconscious, The